Canary as Pets

The Ultimate Canary Care Guide

Canary breeding, diet, cages, singing, where to buy, cost, health, lifespan, types, and more covered!

By Lolly Brown

Foreword

The canary is a bright and cheery little bird that comes in a variety of bold colors ranging from yellow to orange to red. If you are thinking about getting a pet bird, the canary is a great option to consider because it is fairly easy to care for and it is not a social species that needs to be kept with other birds. Before you go out and buy a canary, however, you should learn as much as you can about them to ensure that it truly is the right pet for you and that you are equipped to care for it properly.

If you think that the canary might be the right pet for you, this book is the perfect place to start your journey into bird ownership. In this book you will find a wealth of information about the canary in general as well as specifics regarding care, feeding, breeding, and more. By the time you finish this book you will not only have a deeper understanding of the canary as a pet, but you will know for sure whether or not it is the right pet for you. If it is, the information in this book will have you well on your way to becoming the best canary owner you can be!

Table of Contents

Chapter One: Introduction...1

    Glossary of Important Terms..3

Chapter Two: Understanding Canaries 2

    1.) What Are Canaries?...3

    2.) Facts About Canaries...4

        Summary of Facts...7

    3.) History of Canaries..8

    4.) Types of Canaries..10

Chapter Three: What to Know Before You Buy....................14

    1.) How Many Should You Buy?..................................15

    2.) Can Canaries Be Kept with Other Pets? 16

    3.) Ease and Cost of Care..17

        a.) Initial Costs 17

        b.) Monthly Costs 19

    4.) Pros and Cons of Canaries.......................................22

Chapter Four: Purchasing Canaries..24

    1.) Do You Need a Permit?...25

        1.) U.S. Licensing Requirements...........................25

        2.) U.K. and Australia Permit Requirements.................26

    2.) Where to Buy Canaries..27

        a. Tips for Finding a Canary Breeder 28

b. Canary Breeders in the United States..........................30

c. Canary Breeders in the United Kingdom....................31

3.) How to Select a Healthy Canary.................................31

Chapter Five: Caring for Canaries 34

1.) Habitat Requirements...35

a.) Minimum Cage Requirements 35

b.) Cage Accessories and Toys.....................................37

c.) Building Your Own Cage..41

d.) Lighting and Temperature 42

2.) Feeding Canaries...43

a.) Nutritional Needs of Canaries 44

b.) Types of Food 45

c.) Feeding Tips and Amount to Feed 49

d. Harmful Foods to Avoid..50

3.) Handling and Taming Canaries..................................52

a. Tips for Taming Canaries...52

b.) Trimming Your Canary's Nails 54

c.) Clipping a Canary's Wings......................................55

Chapter Six: Breeding Canaries......................................56

1.) Basic Canary Breeding Info 57

a.) Sexual Dimorphism 57

b.) Courtship Behavior...58

c.) Nest Building 59

2.) The Canary Breeding Process 60

Chapter Seven: Keeping Canaries Healthy 64

1.) Common Health Problems 65

2.) Preventing Illness 74

3.) Quarantining/Introducing New Birds 76

Chapter Eight: Canary Care Sheet 80

1.) Basic Information 81

2.) Cage Set-up Guide 82

3.) Nutritional Information 83

4.) Breeding Tips 84

Chapter Nine: Relevant Websites 86

1. Canary Cage Links 87

2. Canary Cage Accessories and Toys 88

3. Canary Diet and Food Links 90

Index 92

Photo Credits 100

References 104

Chapter One: Introduction

When you hear the word "canary" you probably picture a small, bright yellow bird with a cheery personality. What many people do not realize is that the bird they picture as a canary is just one specific type of canary – there are actually dozens of different species, both wild and domesticated. The wild canary is a member of the finch family and it is usually greenish yellow in color. The domestic canary – the type kept most frequently as a pet – has been selectively bred for its bright yellow coloration, though it comes in other colors as well.

If you are thinking about getting a pet bird, the canary is a great option for beginners. Canaries are medium-sized birds that come in a variety of colors and patterns. The canary is generally easy to care for and it is not a very social bird so you do not have to worry about keeping it with other birds. Canaries can live for up to 20 years, however, so getting a canary is a major commitment – one you need to think carefully about before you make it to ensure that you are fully prepared.

If you think that the canary might be the right pet for you, you would be wise to learn everything you can about the bird before you buy it. In this book you will find a wealth of information about the canary in general as well as specifics regarding care, feeding, breeding, and more. By the time you finish this book you will not only have a deeper understanding of the canary as a pet, but you will know for sure whether or not it is the right pet for you. If it is, the information in this book will have you well on your way to becoming the best canary owner you can be!

To learn more about the canary as a pet and as a species in general, turn the page and keep reading!

Glossary of Important Terms

Avian – Pertaining to birds.

Axillars – The feathers located on the underside at the base of a bird's wing.

Beak – The mouth of a bird consisting of the upper and lower mandibles.

Breast – The chest of a bird located between the chin and the abdomen.

Brood – The offspring of birds.

Chick – A newly hatched bird; a baby bird.

Cloaca – The aperture through which birds excrete; also the location where eggs and sperm exit the body.

Clutch – The eggs laid by a female bird in a single setting.

Down Feathers – The small feathers that keep a bird warm.

Endemic – Referring to a species that is only found in a particular area.

Fledgling – A young bird that is old enough to leave the nest but still largely depends on the parents.

Flight Feathers – Groups of later feathers found on the wing and tail; includes primary, secondary, and tertiary feathers.

Flock – A group of birds.

Genealogy – The history of the descent of a particular species from its ancestors.

Hatching – The process through which baby birds emerge from the egg.

Hatchling - A newly hatched chick.

Hybrid – The offspring of two different species.

Incubation – The act of resting on eggs to generate heat which causes the eggs to eventually hatch.

Molt – The process through which a bird loses its feathers and grows new ones.

Ornithologist – A professional who studies birds.

Pair Bond – The bond formed between a male and female bird for nesting and breeding purposes.

Pinfeathers – The tiny, developing feathers that emerge from the skin.

Remiges – The wing feathers of a bird.

Retrices – The tail feathers of a bird.

Sexual Dimorphism – Referring to physical differences between the sexes of the same species.

Taxonomy – The classification of species into order, family, genera, etc.

Chapter Two: Understanding Canaries

The canary is a beautiful bird that often makes a wonderful pet, though it is not the right option for everyone. Before you can decide whether the canary is the right pet for you, you need to take the time to learn as much as you can about the species. In this chapter you will receive an overview of what the canary is including important facts about the canary's habitat, diet, and breeding requirements. By the time you finish this chapter you will have a deeper understanding of the canary species which will help you to decide if this is the right pet for you.

1.) *What Are Canaries?*

The canary is a small bird belonging to the *Serinus* genus within the finch family. Canaries are often referred to as passerine birds – this simply means that they are a member of the order Passeriformes. This order includes roughly half of all of the bird species in existence including most songbirds. The bird most commonly known as the wild canary is actually the Atlantic canary, *Serinus canaria*. It is also known as the island canary, the common canary, or simply the canary.

In the wild, the canary typically exhibits a yellow-green color with brown streaking on the back. The belly and the area under the tail are usually white with some dark streaks while the rump is a dull yellow color. Females of the species are similar in appearance, though they have duller coloration with a grey head and breast with less yellow coloration. Juvenile canaries have very little yellow coloration at all – they are typically brown in color with dark-colored streaks.

The bird you know as the pet canary is simply a domesticated form of the wild canary. Canaries were bred for the first time in captivity during the 17t century after being brought to Europe by Spanish sailors. As the popularity of these birds increased, selective breeding became very common as an effort to create unique colorations for these birds. Though most people think of canaries as yellow birds, they actually come in a wide range of colors including white, orange, brown, black, and even red. There are also different pattern variations.

Though all pet canaries are domesticated versions of the wild canary, the pet canary is divided into three groups. Color canaries, or color-bred canaries, are selectively bred for specific color mutations. Type canaries are bred for their shape and for specific conformations. Song canaries are bred for their individual song patterns. There are hundreds of different canary varieties in existence which means that the pet owner has plenty of options to choose from.

2.) Facts About Canaries

The domestic canary was first bred in the 17th century from the wild canary, also known as the Atlantic canary. The wild canary can be found in the Macaronesian Islands – it is endemic to the Canary Islands, Morocco, Azores, and Madeira. Wild canaries are most common in the Canary Islands with an estimated population of up to 90,000 pairs. In the Azores, the estimated population is about 60,000 pairs and, in Madeira, it is closer to 5,000 or 6,000 pairs.

The wild canary can be found in a variety of different habitats, though primarily in forested areas. Wild canaries have been known to inhabit pine forests and laurel forests as well as man-made habitats like gardens and parks. Canaries in the wild tend to favor semi-open areas with plenty of small trees, though they are adaptable to a variety of different habitats. In terms of diet, wild canaries feed primarily on seeds and other plant matter as well as various small insects.

Due to selective breeding, there are dozens, even hundreds of different varieties of canary. The wild canary, however, typically stands about 4 to 4.7 inches tall (10 to 12 cm) and weighs an average of 15 grams (0.53 oz.). These birds have an average wingspan of 8 to 9 inches (20 to 32 cm) though it has fairly short wings compared to some of the other species belonging to the same family.

In terms of coloration, the wild canary is primarily yellow-green in color with more yellow than green on the head and face. The lower portion of the belly and the part under the tail is light in color, close to white, with dark streaks along the sides. The upper portion of the body is a grey-green color with dark-colored streaks and the rump is mostly yellow. Female canaries are similar in size and shape but duller in coloration with less yellow. Juveniles of the species are mostly brown with dark streaking.

In the wild, the canary tends to nest in groups with others of its own kind and each breeding pair defends its own small portion of the territory. Canaries build cup-shaped nests about 10 to 13 feet (3 to 4 meters) off the ground. These birds hide their nests amongst the leaves in the trees where they nest, often building them at the end of a branch or in the fork of a branch. Nests are made up of grass, twigs, moss, and other plant material then lined with hair and feathers from the birds.

The nesting period for wild canaries varies a little bit by location. In the Canary Islands, eggs are typically laid between January and July. In Madeira, the nesting season is between March and June with the peak being between April and May. In the Azores, nesting usually occurs between March and July with a spark in May to June.

When the eggs are laid, they are pale blue or bluish-green in color with red or violet-colored markings on the broadest end. Most clutches contain 3 to 4 eggs, though it is possible for a clutch to contain as many as 5 eggs. Most canaries have two to three broods each year and the eggs are incubated for a period of 13 to 14 days. After hatching, the young birds leave the nest after 14 to 21 days, the average being 15 to 17 days. The average lifespan for the canary is 10 to 15 years, though they can live as long as 20 years in captivity. Breeding females sometimes have shorter lifespans closer to 6 years.

Summary of Facts

- **Classification**: *Serinus canaria domestica*
- **Taxonomy**: order Passeriformes, family Fringillidae, genus Serinus, species *Serinus canaria*
- **Distribution**: Macaronesian Islands (Canary Islands, Morocco, Azores, and Madeira)
- **Habitat**: forested areas, primarily pine and laurel forests; also man-made habitats
- **Anatomical Adaptations**:
- **Eggs**: up to 5 per clutch, average is 3 to 4; 2 to 3 broods per year
- **Incubation Period**: average 13 to 14 days
- **Hatchling**: young birds leave the next after 14 to 21 days, average 15 to 17 days
- **Average Size**: 4 to 4.7 inches in length (10 to 12 cm)
- **Average Weight**: 15 grams (0.53 oz.)
- **Wingspan**: about 8 to 9 inches (20 to 23 cm)

- **Coloration**: wide variety of colors; yellow, white, orange, red, black, brown, etc.
- **Sexual Dimorphism**: male is more brightly colored; female has a greyer head
- **Diet**: mostly seeds, small insects, and other plant materials
- **Vocalization**: silvery twittering, similar to some finches
- **Lifespan**: average 10 to 15 years

3.) History of Canaries

The wild canary was first classified in 1758 by Linnaeus and it was identified as a subspecies of the European serin within the *Fringilla* genus. Several decades later, Cuvier reclassified the canary into the *Serinus* genus and that is where they remain today. The closest relative of the canary is still the European serin and the two species are capable of hybridizing. There is a 25% fertility rate for hybrids of these two species.

The name "canary" comes from the bird's native habitat, the Canary Islands. The name of the islands was taken from the Latin, *canariae insulae*, or "islands of dogs". This name was given in reference to the large dogs that many native islanders kept. There is another legend that suggests that conquistadors named the islands after a fierce island tribe known as the "Canarii". It is unclear how much truth there is to this theory.

For many years, canaries were used in coal mining operations as a warning system for toxic gases. Gasses like methane, carbon dioxide, and carbon monoxide are very common in mines and these gasses would kill the canary before they started to affect the miners. Before the days of chemical detection, miners would monitor the canary – any signs of distress would be taken as an indication of unsafe conditions. This practice continued throughout Europe until the late 1980s.

Today, canaries are primarily kept as pets, though they have been used in some important scientific research as well. Fernando Nottebohm, a professor from Rockefeller University in New York City used canaries to study the structure and pathways of the brain in relation to bird song. Canaries have also been used in studies of neurogenesis, the production of new neurons in the brain. They have also been used as a model for studying how the animal brain learns, recalls motor movements, and records memories.

4.) Types of Canaries

As you have already learned, domestic canaries can be divided into three categories: color canaries, type canaries, and song canaries. Color canaries are bred for specific color mutations while type canaries are bred for their shape and for specific conformations. Song canaries are bred for their individual song patterns. In this section you will receive an overview of some of the most popular species in each group.

Color Canaries

A canary's color is derived from two types of color – melanin color and lipochrome color. The lipochrome color is also known as the "ground color", or the more dominant color. In the wild canary, the lipochrome color is the yellow or green color. The melanin color includes the darker hues like brown and black. When combined together, the lipochrome and melanin colors produce different variations like green, bronze, fawn, cinnamon, blue, and brown. The Red Factor canary is thought to be the result of crossing a canary with a Red-Hooded Siskin, a bird that is very rare and endangered in the wild.

Types of color canaries include:
- Color Bred Canary (yellow, orange, green, blue, brown, bronze, etc.)
- Red Factor Canary

Type Canaries

The canaries belonging to this group have been selectively bred for certain characteristics such as size, shape, or feathers. Some type canaries are bred for extreme characteristics like frills or swooping feather patterns.

Varieties of type canaries include:
- Belgian Fancy Canary
- Border Fancy Canary
- Crested Canary
- Fife Fancy Canary
- Gloster Fancy Canary

- Lizard Canary
- Northern Dutch Frilled Canary
- Norwich Canary
- Parisian Frilled Canary
- Stafford Canary
- Yorkshire Canary

Song Canaries

These canaries are bred specifically for their songs. Some canary songs are trilling and sweet while others are loud, almost metallic-sounding.

Types of song canaries include:
- American Singer Canary
- Hartz Roller Canary
- Persian Singer Canary
- Russian Singer Canary
- Spanish Timbrado
- Waterslager Canary

Chapter Three: What to Know Before You Buy

Now that you have a better understanding of what the canary is you are well on your way to deciding whether or not these birds are the right pet for you. In this chapter you will receive some important and practical information about being a canary owner. You will learn whether canaries should be kept individually or in pairs, whether they can be kept with other pets, and what the average cost to own a canary is. By considering the information in this chapter you will be able to make an informed decision regarding whether these are the right pets for you.

1.) How Many Should You Buy?

One of the first questions new canary owners ask is whether they can keep multiple canaries together or if it is better to keep them singly. Although the canary is a type of finch, canaries are much less of a social species than most finches. This being the case, it is generally recommended that you keep only a single canary or a breeding pair. If you try to keep multiple male canaries together you will just be asking for trouble.

It is possible for two male canaries to get along outside of the breeding season but eventually you will run into problems with dominance. Not only will keeping multiple canaries likely result in dominance issues, but it can also reduce the amount your canaries are likely to sing. It is only the male of the species that sings but keeping multiple males together can interfere with that singing. If you must keep multiple canaries together, a mixed-gender grouping is better than keeping just males.

If you do plan to keep multiple canaries it is essential that you have a very large cage. Make sure there are plenty of perches and nests in the cage so each canary can have its own territory. Something that many canary owners find to be effective is a very large shared flight cage connected to multiple smaller units which individual canaries can claim as their territory. This type of cage setup can be expensive and a hassle to keep clean but it generally works as far as keeping multiple canaries amicable with each other.

2.) Can Canaries Be Kept with Other Pets?

Because canaries are generally supposed to be kept in their cages at all times it is possible to keep canaries in households with other pets. As long as your canary cage is out of reach for dogs, cats, and other animals that might bother the birds, you shouldn't have a problem. The real question, however, is whether you can keep canaries with other birds. Canaries are members of the finch family, so many canary owners wonder whether or not these birds can be kept together.

Although canaries are closely related to finches, the two cannot always be kept together. Finches come in a wide variety of shapes and sizes and some species are more social than others. If you do want to keep canaries and finches together, be sure to choose species of similar size and make sure that the finches you choose are a passive species like society finches. Zebra finches and other species tend to be a little more pushy and aggressive so they may not get along with canaries. You should not keep canaries with parrots or parakeets due to differences in feeding and handling requirements.

3.) Ease and Cost of Care

Owning a pet can be expensive so before you make the commitment you need to be sure that you can cover the necessary costs. For a pet canary you need to not only be able to pay for the canary itself, but you also need to provide a safe and healthy habitat as well as a healthy diet. In this section you will receive an overview of the costs associated with purchasing and keeping a canary as a pet. If you cannot cover these costs, a canary might not be the right pet for you.

a.) Initial Costs

The initial costs associated with keeping canaries as pets include the cost of the bird itself as well as the cage, cage accessories, toys, and grooming supplies. You will find an overview of these costs below as well as a chart depicting the estimated costs for keeping a single canary as well as a pair of canaries:

Purchase Price – The average cost for a canary will vary a little bit depending on the age, the variety, and where you get it. Depending what type of canary you get, you should plan to spend $50 to $200 (£45 to £180).

Cage – The cost for a high-quality canary cage will vary greatly depending on the size, the type of cage, and the quality of the materials. Your best option is a large flight cage which could cost anywhere from $75 to as much as $500 or more (£68 to £450).

Cage Accessories – To properly outfit your canary cage you will need at least three food and water dishes as well as a nesting box, and several perches. The cost for these items can vary greatly but you should budget about $100 to $200 (£90 to £180) to be safe.

Toys – You really only need to keep 3 toys in your canary's cage at any given time, though you should keep a variety of toys on hand so you can rotate them in and out to prevent bored. Plan to spend about $50 (£45) on toys.

Grooming Supplies – Like many birds, canaries enjoy taking baths so you will need to have a bird bath available in your canary cage. Other grooming supplies you might need include tail trimmers, styptic powder and wing clippers. The average cost you can expect to pay for these supplies is around $40 (£36).

Initial Costs for Canaries		
Cost Type	**1 Canary**	**2 Canaries**
Purchase Price	$50 to $200 (£45 to £180)	$100 to $400 (£90 to £360)
Cage	$75 to $500 (£68 to £450)	$75 to $500 (£68 to £450)
Accessories	$100 to $200 (£90 to £180)	$100 to $200 (£90 to £180)
Toys	$50 (£45)	$100 (£90)
Grooming Supplies	$40 (£36)	$40 (£36)
Total	$315 to $990 (£284 to £891)	$415 to $1,240 (£374 to £1,116)

b.) Monthly Costs

The monthly costs associated with keeping canaries as pets include the cost of bird food, nesting and bedding supplies, cleaning supplies, and veterinary care. You will find an overview of these costs below as well as a chart depicting the estimated costs for keeping a single canary as well as a pair of canaries:

Bird Food – Feeding your canary a high-quality diet is the key to keeping your bird happy and healthy. Some canary owners choose to feed their birds a seed mix while others prefer pellet foods. In addition to your canary's staple diet you should also offer supplemental foods like fresh fruits and vegetables. The cost for canary food varies depending on quality but you should plan to spend about $10 (£9) on a small bag of bird food that will last you about a month. Add to that the cost of fresh and supplemental foods you should budget for about $30 (£27) per month on food.

Nesting/Bedding Supplies – In order for your canary to be able to build a nest you need to provide nesting materials like wood shavings and small twigs. Plan to spend about $15 (£13.50) on nesting supplies.

Cleaning Supplies – If you want to keep your canary healthy you need to maintain a clean cage. You won't need to buy cleaning supplies every month but you should budget a cost of about $10 (£9) per month on supplies.

Veterinary Care – Not all veterinarians are qualified to care for birds so you might have to find an exotics vet to take care of your canary. The average cost for this kind of veterinarian visit is about $50 (£45). You will not need to take your canary to the vet every month. If you take your canary to the vet twice a year and divide that cost over twelve months you should budget about $8 (£7.20) per month.

Additional Costs – In addition to all of these monthly costs you should plan for occasional extra costs like repairs to your canary cage, replacement toys, etc. Again, you won't have to cover these costs every month but you should budget about $10 (£9) per month to be safe.

Monthly Costs for Canaries		
Cost Type	**1 Canary**	**2 Canaries**
Bird Food	$30 (£27)	$60 (£54)
Nesting/Bedding	$15 (£13.50)	$15 (£13.50)
Cleaning Supplies	$10 (£9)	$10 (£9)
Veterinary Care	$8 (£7.20)	$16 (£14.40)
Additional Costs	$10 (£9)	$10 (£9)
Total	$73 (£66)	$111 (£100)

4.) Pros and Cons of Canaries

Before you decide whether or not canaries are the right pet for you, you should familiarize yourself with both the advantages and disadvantages of canaries as a pet. Below you will find a list of pros and cons for canaries to help you make your decision:

Pros for Canaries as Pets

- Canaries remain fairly small, around 4 to 8 inches (10 to 20 cm) so they take up less space than parrots.
- Male canaries can sing and individual species have unique songs.

- Canaries are generally a passive species, not likely to bite when handled.
- Very active species, can be entertaining to keep.
- Canaries come in a wide range of colors and patterns, some with unique feathering.
- Compared to many pet birds, canaries are a low-maintenance option.

Cons for Canaries as Pets

- Many canaries are messy eaters, flinging seed around the cage – may also be picky eaters.
- Some canaries can be very loud.
- Canaries are very active, they require very large cages with plenty of space for flying.
- May not be the best species if you want a bird that you can handle frequently.
- Generally not recommended for keeping with other birds except some passive finch species.

Chapter Four: Purchasing Canaries

In the previous chapter you received the kind of practical information you need to know about keeping canaries as pets. If you still feel like the canary is the right option for you, congratulations! You are almost ready to become a canary owner. The information in this chapter will help you learn where to get a canary, whether you need a permit to keep one, and how to choose a healthy canary from a breeder. All of this information is very important in order to ensure that the canary you buy is in good health.

1.) Do You Need a Permit?

Before you bring home any kind of new pet you need to make sure that there aren't any legal restrictions in your area. Some pets are illegal to keep without a permit or license, so you need to be very careful. In this section you will learn the basics about permit requirements for keeping canaries as pets.

1.) U.S. Licensing Requirements

The United States has a lot of laws governing which animals are and are not legal to keep. In most cases, however, these laws apply to endangered or dangerous animals, not so much to pet birds. The one piece of legislation you will need to reference is the Migratory Bird Treaty Act which was passed in 1918. This act states that it is "illegal for anyone to take, possess, import, export, transport, sell, purchase, barter, or offer for sale, purchase, or barter, any migratory bird, or the parts, nests, or eggs of such a bird except under the terms of a valid permit issued pursuant to Federal regulations".

The most important thing you need to take away from this is that it is illegal to keep birds that are native to the United States as pets unless you obtain a special permit. This applies to a number of finch species including the

American Goldfinch, the Purple Finch, and the House Finch. Fortunately, the canary is not a species that is native to the United States. This means that you can keep canaries legally without a permit.

One more thing you need to be wary of with keeping canaries as pets is that they need to be captive-bred. It is not legal to keep wild-caught birds as pets. If you need more information about keeping canaries legally or about obtaining a permit for a wild-caught canary you will need to contact your local branch for the U.S Fish and Wildlife Service. You can find more information about importing and exporting pet birds here:

http://www.fws.gov/international/travel-and-trade/traveling-with-your-pet-bird.html#3

2.) U.K. and Australia Permit Requirements

The laws for keeping certain pets in the U.K. and Australia are very different than the laws in the United States. Just like in the U.S., it is illegal to keep dangerous and endangered animals as pets without a permit, but there are fewer pet regulations in the U.K. in general. You should not need a license or permit to purchase or keep a pet canary because it is neither an endangered nor a native species. The one permit you might need is called an animal movement license – this is the permit you'll need to import, export, or travel with your canary. This requirement is in place to prevent the spread of disease. It is primarily geared toward preventing rabies (the U.K. eradicated rabies a number of years ago) but it applies to other communicable diseases as well.

2.) Where to Buy Canaries

Once you have determined whether it is legal to keep canaries as pets in your area, your next step is to decide where you want to buy your canary. You may or may not be able to find pet canaries at your local pet store and, even if you do, you might want to consider buying directly from a breeder instead. Below you will find some recommendations for finding a reputable canary breeder to ensure that your pet canary is healthy.

a. Tips for Finding a Canary Breeder

Even if you do not buy your canary from a pet store, it is not a bad place to start your search. If the store does carry canaries you can ask them where the birds came from and then contact the supplier for more information. If the store doesn't carry canaries you can ask around to see if they have any information about local breeders. You can also try asking around among your fellow bird lovers or simply perform an online search.

Once you've come up with a list of several canary breeders you want to take the time to vet them. If you are careful about weeding out the hobby breeders from the ones that know what they are doing you are more likely to end up with a healthy, well-bred bird. Keep in mind that canaries come in a wide range of colors, patterns, and feather types so breeders are likely to specialize in a particular type. It will help you to narrow your search if you decide ahead of time which kind of canary you want then you can focus only on breeders for that type.

After assembling and narrowing down your list to include just a handful of options, take the time to review the websites for each breeder. Look for important information about the breeder's experience with canaries and with breeding birds – you should also check to make sure they have the appropriate breeding license, if required in your area. Any breeders that do not appear to have a solid background should be removed from your list before you move to the next step.

Once you've determined that the breeders on your list are qualified and experienced you should call them individually and ask them some important questions. When speaking directly to the breeder you can gain important information about their breeding practices to determine whether or not they really know what they are doing. Any breeder that refuses to answer questions or that cannot answer your questions fully and confidently should be removed from your list.

By this point you should have narrowed down your list to two or three breeders. The next step is to actually visit the breeding facilities to make sure that the breeder is actually doing what he says he is. Ask for a tour of the facilities to make sure that they are clean and well-kept – you should also ask to see the breeding stock to make sure that they are in good health and that they are good examples of the type you are seeking. After this visit you should be able to narrow down your options to just one breeder at which point you can actually purchase your canary or put down a deposit if the birds are not old enough to go home yet.

b. Canary Breeders in the United States

Below you will find links to several canary breeders in the United States:

Dian's Color Bred Canaries. <http://myredcanary.com/>

Ginger's Song Canaries. <http://wolnik.us/canary/>

John Kotsoros. <http://www.johnkotsoros.com/en/ historique.htm>

The House of Glosters. <http://www.thehouseofglosters. com/>

Spanish Timbrado Song Canary Breeder List. <http://spanishtimbrado.us/Breeder_List.html>

Canadian Roller Canary Breeder List. <http://www.germanroller.com/canadian_roller_canary_bre eders.html>

c. Canary Breeders in the United Kingdom

<u>Below you will find links to several canary breeders in the United Kingdom</u>:

Canary Colour Breeders Association.
<http://www.colourcanaries.co.uk/main_page.html>

Richard Lumley Gloster Canaries.
<http://www.richardlumley.co.uk/>

Jeff Hamlett's Fife Canaries. <http://www.fifecanary.co.uk/breeding1.htm>

Steve Dominey Yorkshire & Fife Fancy Canaries.
<http://www.stevedomineycanaries.co.uk/#/bird-room/4572345796>

3.) How to Select a Healthy Canary

Choosing a reputable breeder will help to ensure that the canary you bring home is well-bred but you still need to take certain steps to ensure that it is healthy as well. While it is certainly possible to buy a canary sight unseen, it is not recommended. Canaries can live for 10 years or more when properly cared for, so you want to make sure that your pet canary has the best start to its life as possible. Follow the steps below to make sure you come home from the breeder with a healthy canary:

- Observe the bird from afar before approaching it – you want to make sure that it exhibits a healthy activity level and that it is able to sit on the perch properly.

- Examine the bird's body language – does it appear healthy and active? Does it seem to be overly shy or frightened of humans? Are there any visible signs of illness?

- If possible, watch the bird fly and eat to make sure that both of these functions can be performed normally without any problems.

- Check the state of the cage the canary is kept in – is it clean? Are the food/water bowls clean?

- Take a closer look at the canary to look for signs of illness – are its eyes bright and clear? Are its feathers puffed up? Are there patches of dirty or lost feathers?

- Once you've determined that there are no obvious signs of illness, take a moment to handle the canary if it will let you – use this opportunity to examine the bird more closely.

- Check the vent (the area under the tail) for cleanliness – if the area is dirty it could be a sign of diarrhea which is a sign of illness in birds.

- Examine the bird's feathers to make sure they have grown in properly and that they are the right color, pattern, or type that you prefer.

If everything about the bird appears to be healthy you can speak to the breeder about putting down a deposit or take the bird home immediately. Make sure to ask whether the bird comes with any sort of health guarantee or documentation that you might need.

Chapter Five: Caring for Canaries

Being a canary owner is a wonderful experience but it does require a good deal of planning and forethought. Your canary will be completely dependent on you to provide for his needs so you should take the time to learn about your canary's requirements for habitat, feeding, and handling. In this chapter you will receive a wealth of knowledge about setting up your canary's cage, creating a healthy diet for your canary, and tips for properly handling your pet bird. Be sure to review this information carefully before you commit to buying a canary – if you can't provide for your canary's needs you should find another pet.

1.) Habitat Requirements

One of the most important things you need to do as a canary owner is to provide your canary with a safe and healthy habitat. Pet birds spend most of their lives in their cage so choosing the right cage is not a decision that should be taken lightly. In this section you will receive in-depth instructions regarding the selection and accessorizing of your canary's cage.

a.) Minimum Cage Requirements

In the wild, canaries tend to prefer open or semi-open spaces so you should plan to provide your canary with a fairly large cage. If you are tempted to save money by purchasing a smaller cage, keep in mind that your canary will spend almost his entire life in the cage – it is worth getting a bigger cage to make sure that he is happy and healthy. Canaries are not very large birds, so a cage that is roomy enough for a canary still won't be as large as a cage for a parrot or another bird would be – keep that in mind as well.

For a single canary, the minimum cage size is 18 inches wide, 18 inches deep, and about 24 inches tall (46x46x61 cm). This is the minimum recommendation for a single canary in order to allow normal flight patterns. If you plan to keep more than one canary in the same cage, you will want it to be a little bit bigger. The best thing you can do for your canary is to buy something called a flight cage. A flight cage is simply a cage that is large enough and long enough to allow for normal flight.

While size is the most important factor for your canary's cage, there are a few other things you need to consider. For example, the spacing between the bars on your canary's cage is very important. You want to spacing to be no more than ½ inch – if the spacing is any large your canary could get its head caught between the bars or he could even escape. Bars spaced too far apart could also impact your canary's ability to perch and climb on the sides of the cage.

Another factor you want to consider is the bottom of the cage. Your canary will spend most of his time flying around the cage and resting on his perches, but you do need to think about the bottom of the cage as well. It is best to find a cage that has a slide-out tray at the bottom to facilitate easy cleaning. You can line this tray with newspaper or bird cage liners and then just throw it away and replace it for quick cleaning. The actual bottom of the cage can be completely open or it can be made up of metal wire mesh. Wire grill on the bottom of the cage will help to keep your canary's feet clean if he lands on the floor.

b.) Cage Accessories and Toys

In addition to providing your canary with a cage large enough for him to fly in, you also need to provide certain cage accessories. Not only do you need to provide your canary with certain accessories, but you have to be intentional about how you arrange the cage as well. The most important cage accessories for a pet canary include the following:

- Food and water dishes
- Perches
- Bathing tub
- Nesting box
- Nesting materials
- Cuttlebone
- Toys

Food and Water Dishes

Food and water should be available to your canary at all times and the number of dishes you need will depend on the number of canaries you are keeping. If you have more than one canary you'll need a separate food dish for each as well as one or two water dishes. The dishes should be made of sturdy materials because your canary will perch on them to eat and drink – stainless steel is the best option because it is the easier to clean and it won't harbor bacteria. Ceramic dishes are another good option, though they are heavier and might be more difficult to mount in the cage. Many canary owners recommend having multiple separate bowls for different types of food – one for water, one for pellets or seed mix, and one for fresh foods.

Perches

Though canaries spend a lot of time flying, they need access to perches when they want to rest. You should provide your canary with at least three different perches made from different materials like natural wood or wooden dowels. Avoid plastic perches because they can get scratched up and then might harbor bacteria. Look for perches that offer some kind of texture so the canary will be able to grip it – do not use perches that are completely smooth. Perches should be about ¼ to ½ inch in diameter for canaries.

Bathing Tub

Canaries like to bathe because it helps them to remove debris from their feathers and it helps to keep their skin moisturized as well. For small birds like the canary you can keep a bird bath in the cage so the bird can bathe whenever it likes. The bird bath should consist of a shallow, heavy bowl filled with 1 or 2 inches of water – the water should not be deeper than the height of your canary. Keep an eye on the bird bath and refresh the water after each bath. You can go with a bird bath that sits on the bottom of the cage or you can go with one that mounts to the side of the cage. It is simply a matter of preference.

Nesting Box

Canaries breed fairly readily in captivity so you should provide them with a nesting box and nesting materials. The best nesting boxes for canaries are made from wood or bamboo – these materials are soft enough that they won't injure your canary's feet if they get caught. You should mount the nesting box to the back or side of the cage near the top so it doesn't get in the way of your canary's natural flight path.

Nesting Materials

In addition to providing your canary with a nesting box you need to provide him with nesting materials to actually build his nest. Mount a tray or pan of nesting materials to the side of the cage and fill it with soft wood shavings, small twigs, and other soft materials. Make sure the tray you use to hold the materials is sturdy enough to support the weight of your canary and it is best made from easy-to-clean materials like ceramic or stainless steel.

Cuttlebone

Mounting a cuttlebone on the side of your canary cage is highly recommended. Not only will your canary use it as a kind of plaything, but it is also a valuable source of calcium for your bird. As your canary nibbles on the bone it will also help to keep his beak trimmed down.

Toys

In addition to being very active birds, canaries also have a playful side so you'll want to provide your bird with an assortment of toys. Provide your canary with at least three different types of toys and space them throughout the cage so they don't interfere with your canary's flight. Some good options for toys include rope toys, stainless steel bells, swings, and more. Just make sure that your canary toys are made from nontoxic materials that are easy to clean. You may want to keep a large selection of toys and rotate them in and out of the cage to prevent boredom.

Now that you know what accessories your canary needs you can start to think about how you will arrange the cage to accommodate all of them. Canaries are active birds so the most important thing you need to remember is that space for flight is an absolute necessity. You do not want to overcrowd the cage with toys and accessories which might limit your canary's flight.

Try to space your accessories out to leave plenty of open space. One way to do this is to stagger the spacing of your perches and other accessories. For example, you might place two perches along the sides of the cage on either end and then place another set of perches on the front and back walls of the cage higher up. By staggering the perches this way you leave enough room between them for your canary to fly back and forth.

c.) Building Your Own Cage

Because canaries are such an active species they require a large flight cage to remain happy and healthy. Unfortunately, large bird cages can be fairly expensive – especially if you buy one made from high-quality materials. For this reason, many canary owners choose to build their own cages. A DIY canary cage gives you the ability to customize the size and shape of the cage to fit the space you have available in your home. Plus, you can design it to suit the preferences of your canary.

The best materials to use for a DIY canary cage are plywood and welded wire mesh. You can use a sheet of plywood for the top and bottom of the cage then construct the walls out of 1-by-2 inch boards or something similar. You can then use the welded wire mesh to enclose the cage. You also have the option of building wooden accessories like perches and nesting boxes directly into the framework of the cage. Just be sure that all wood surfaces are properly sanded to avoid injury and make sure that the gauge of your welded wire mesh is large enough that your canary's toes won't get caught.

d.) Lighting and Temperature

The size and shape of your canary cage is incredibly important, but you also have to think about the location of the cage as well. Canaries are adaptable to different temperatures, though they prefer warm environments no more than 78°F (25.5°C). The best daytime temperature range for canaries is between 60°F and 70°F (15.5°C to 21°C) with nighttime temperatures dropping no lower than about 40°F (4.5°C).

You may also want to keep an eye on the humidity in your canary's cage. The native habitat of these birds is semi-tropical so you don't need to keep the humidity too high – something in the 50% to 60% range should be sufficient. You can keep the humidity in your canary cage up by misting it with warm water from a spray bottle daily or you can set up a drip system. Higher humidity levels may be beneficial for breeding and for making sure that the eggs do not dry out before hatching.

Place your canary cage in a location that won't be affected by drafts – this means you'll have to keep it away from air conditioning vents, windows, and doors to the outside. The best location for a canary cage is one where the temperature is stable and there is a moderate amount of activity – don't make your canary's cage the center of attention in a very busy room because it could cause stress. If your canary starts to become stressed you can try covering the cage with a blanket or cage cover.

2.) Feeding Canaries

Unfortunately, many bird owners fail to learn even the basics about bird nutrition - they simply offer their birds some seeds and call it a day. While seeds are the primary component of a canary's diet, there is more you should know about your canary's nutritional needs in order to keep him happy and healthy. In this section you will learn the basics about nutritional requirements for canaries and you will receive tips for feeding your own canary.

a.) Nutritional Needs of Canaries

In order to keep your canary healthy you need to understand the basics about his nutritional needs and design a diet that will meet them. In the wild, canaries feed largely on a wide variety of seeds, so that is what you should feed your pet canary. It is important to remember, however, that seeds are not the only things wild canaries eat – they also feed on small insects and certain fruits, vegetables, and berries.

For canaries, about 60% to 70% of the diet should be made up of seeds but there are some other important foods to include as well. In addition to seeds, your canary should receive small amounts of fresh fruits and vegetables as well as some cooked grains and other supplementary foods. You may also want to give your canary some dietary supplements to help round out his nutrition.

In addition to feeding your canary a well-balanced diet, you should also make sure that fresh water is always available. Not only is fresh water important for keeping your canary hydrated but it will also help to ensure healthy digestion. Most canaries will drink water from a small bowl or dish mounted on the side of the cage. Just keep an eye on it and refresh the water daily, cleaning the bowl when you do to get rid of food particles and germs.

b.) Types of Food

In the wild, canaries feed on a variety of different seeds, but mostly grass seeds. You can certainly put together your own seed mix if you want to, but it will be easier to just purchase a high-quality canary seed mix. Purchasing a commercial seed mix is usually the easier option, but you do need to be careful about which blend you choose. Some seed mixes are too high in fats and carbohydrates but low in protein and other nutrients. Look for a seed mix that provides a good balance of nutrients without being too high in fat.

Another problem you might run into with commercial seed mixes is that the canary could simply pick out its favorite seeds, leaving the rest untouched. For example, many canaries favor millet seed and they will pick them out of the seed mix. If you are worried about this happening to you, consider buying a canary pellet food instead of a seed blend. Canary pellets are made primarily from seed, but the ingredients are all blended together which means that your bird can't pick out certain seeds that he likes. Canary pellet foods also contain supplemental ingredients like grains and proteins to ensure well-rounded nutrition for your bird.

While a seed mix or canary pellet is the best option for your canary's staple diet, 30% to 40% of his diet should consist of other foods. Your canary will get plenty of healthy nutrition from fresh fruits and vegetables as well as whole grain bread, cooked rice or sweet potato, sprouted seeds, and mealworms or other insects. You might also want to consider offering your canary a cuttlebone to make sure he gets the minerals he needs.

Fresh Vegetables (offer daily)

• Beets	• Kale
• Bean Sprouts	• Lettuce
• Broccoli*	• Parsley
• Carrot	• Peas
• Carrot Tops	• Pumpkin
• Corn	• Spinach*
• Collard Greens	• Sweet Potato
• Cucumber	• Yams
• Dandelion Greens	• Zucchini

*Only offer these foods once or twice a week because they could interfere with calcium uptake.

Fresh Fruits (3x per week)

- Apple
- Apricots
- Banana
- Blueberries
- Kiwi
- Grapes
- Oranges
- Peaches
- Pears
- Raspberries

Grains and Starch (2x per week)

- Whole grain bread
- Whole wheat bread
- Cooked brown rice
- Cook sweet potato
- Cooked white potato
- Soaked/sprouted seeds

Protein (2x per week)

- Cooked chicken egg
- Mealworms

Supplements

Fresh fruits and vegetables will help to round out your canary's nutrition but you should also provide certain supplements to make sure his needs for certain vitamins and minerals are being met. One option is to provide your canary with a cuttlefish bone, also known as a cuttlebone – this is a great source of calcium. Many canary owners also provide their birds with oyster grit. Oyster grit contains both calcium and phosphorus, plus it can help your bird to digest fibrous foods and seeds.

You can also find multivitamin powders that you can mix directly into your canary's water but it is a good idea to ask your vet first to make sure you aren't over-supplementing your canary. It is possible to have too much of a good thing and overdosing on certain nutrients could be harmful for your bird.

Soaked and Sprouted Seeds

Soaked seeds can be considered an occasional treat for canaries, though they are an essential food for feeding hens and newly weaned hatchlings. Large seeds like wheat, cracked corn, buckwheat, and safflower are usually too much for canaries to handle but soaking them makes them easier to eat – it actually helps to start breaking down the complex carbohydrates to make them more digestible. Soak seeds for at least 24 hours and rinse then strain them well before offering them to your canary.

Sprouted seeds are not the same thing as soaked seeds and not all seeds can be sprouted. Mung beans are the easiest seeds to sprout and they are considered very palatable for canaries and other birds. You can also use soy beans but most birds do not like alfalfa sprouts. To sprout seeds, place no more than a quarter cup in a clean glass jar then fill with tap water. Let the jar set for 24 hours at room temperature then rinse and drain. Rinse and drain the seeds once daily until the seeds have sprouted – discard them if they develop a mold or foul odor at any time. Sprouted seeds can be kept fresh in the refrigerator for up to two weeks before discarding them.

c.) Feeding Tips and Amount to Feed

The best way to feed your canary is to keep one or more seed dishes in the cage. Make sure not to fill the dishes too full because your canary could soil the dishes, ruining the food, and you don't want to waste too much of it. Check your seed dishes at least twice daily to make sure they are clean and refill them as needed with fresh pellets. To offer your canary fresh fruits and vegetables, place them in a separate dish or clip them to the side of the cage.

In terms of how much food you should be offering your canary, recommendations vary. As a general guideline, start with 1 to 2 level teaspoons of seed or pellets per bird per day. If you have more than one canary in the same cage, make sure there is at least one food dish per bird and space them out so each bird can eat in peace. If you choose to use canary pellets, refer to the feeding recommendations on the package. You want to avoid overfeeding your canary because these birds are prone to obesity if they are overfed.

If you start out feeding your canary seeds, it may be difficult for you to switch him over to a pelleted diet later. The best way to do this is to slowly wean your canary off the seeds while making sure that pellet foods are constantly available. If you choose this method you should do it over a period of 6 to 8 weeks to make sure that you don't make any major changes to your canary's diet too quickly. You can also try mixing a little bit of the pelleted food in with your seeds to get your canary used to it.

When feeding your canary fresh fruits and vegetables it is essential that you clean them properly. In addition to washing your produce, remove any pits or seeds and chop the foods into small, manageable pieces before offering them to your canary. It is a good idea to have a separate food dish for fresh foods because if you put it in with the seed it could encourage mold or fungus growth when the seeds get wet.

d. Harmful Foods to Avoid

Though many so-called "people foods" like fresh fruits and whole grain bread can be good for your canary, many are not. Avoid feeding your canary dairy products, sugary foods, salty foods, raw potato, beans, and canned foods. It is also important to note that while certain vegetables like lettuce and cabbage are not necessarily bad for your bird, they are very high in water and offer relatively little in the way of nutritional value. There are also some foods that are considered toxic or harmful for canaries – you will find them listed here below:

- Asparagus
- Avocado
- Alcohol
- Caffeine
- Chocolate
- Cocoa
- Dried Beans
- Eggplant
- Fruit Pits

- Fruit Seeds
- Poultry Feed
- Raw Egg
- Rhubarb
- Tobacco
- Tomato
- Milk
- Moldy Foods
- Mushrooms

**It is also important to note that even safe foods need to be clean and free from mold. Do not feed your canary anything that is damp, moldy, or anything less than fresh.

3.) Handling and Taming Canaries

For the most part, canaries are kept for their lovely appearance and their beautiful singing. In most cases, canary owners keep their birds in the cage without letting them out. If you plan to show your canary, however, you may need to train and tame your canary so that it can be let out of its cage. Keep in mind that canaries are fairly timid creatures so it could take a long time to train or tame a canary and it is best to start when they are very young.

a. Tips for Taming Canaries

If you want to have a tamed canary that will allow you to handle it, you should start with a very young bird and it is recommended that you keep only one. The proper way to handle a canary is to place your hand gently on its back and wrap your fingers around the bird's body with your thumb and forefinger circled around the head and neck for support. Be careful not to hold the canary too tightly but maintain a firm enough grip that it won't be able to get away.

For the best results, start with a canary that is less than 6 months of age. Look for a bird that exhibits an active curiosity – you don't want to pick a canary that is overly timid or shy because it will take a lot longer to tame and train a shy bird. Once you've picked your canary you should start with a daily training routine consisting of two 10- to 15-minute sessions. Make sure to hold these training sessions at the same time each day so your canary gets used to the routine.

Before you even handle your canary for the first time you need to get it used to you. Start by placing your hands in the cage, holding them out flat like a perch. You may even want to place a treat in your hand to encourage your bird to land there. Keep your hand steady and just wait for your canary to come around – do not chase him around the cage. If he doesn't come to you after 10 or 15 minutes, remove your hands and try again later. As long as you are patient and consistent you will eventually be successful in taming your canary. In terms of training, canaries can be taught to perform simple tricks. Again, it will take a great deal of time and patience to achieve this goal, so be prepared for that before you begin.

If you plan to handle your canary on a regular basis you need to be able to recognize signs of stress in your bird. You should only handle your canary for short periods of time and as soon as he starts to get uncomfortable it is best to put him back in the cage. Signs of stress in canaries may include flattening the feathers against the body, panting with the mouth open, or moving away from you. Canaries generally do not bite but if you continue holding your canary while he is becoming increasingly stressed it could induce this kind of behavior.

b.) Trimming Your Canary's Nails

Trimming your canary's nails is a necessary task but it can also be a challenging one. For one thing, some canaries simply do not like being held so if your canary isn't tamed and used to handling, trimming his nails could become quite the ordeal. When it comes time to trim your bird's nails, hold him using the method described in the last section. Carefully maneuver your hand to hold one toe between your thumb and forefinger then clip just the very tip of the nail. Keep in mind that each nail contains a quick - that is the blood vessel that supplies blood to the nail. If you clip the nail too short you could sever the quick and that will be painful for your canary.

Even if you are very careful when cutting your canary's nails there is always the risk that you might cut the quick. If you do, the nail could start bleeding profusely and that is something you want to get under control right away. You can stop the bleeding quickly by dipping the nail in cornstarch, flour, or styptic powder. Always keep one of these materials on hand when you clip your canary's nails, just in case you need it. If you aren't confident in your ability to cut your canary's nails try having a veterinarian show you how.

c.) Clipping a Canary's Wings

Keeping a pet canary is not like keeping a pet parrot. While pet parrots and other larger birds can be allowed out of the cage, canaries generally spend most of their lives in the cage. The only reason you would need to clip a bird's wings is if it is allowed out of the cage and you want to limit its flight. For canaries, being able to fly is incredibly important because they are very active birds. If you clip your canary's wings you would impede his ability to fly and it could have a negative impact on his health and overall wellbeing.

Chapter Six: Breeding Canaries

Canaries are generally a solitary species so they do not need to be kept in large groups like finches and other pet birds. If you do decide to keep two canaries together, however, you should be prepared for the possibility of breeding – especially if you keep a male and a female together. If you are interested in breeding your canaries you will be glad to know that canaries breed fairly readily and they do not require a great deal of specialized care. In this chapter you will learn the basics about breeding canaries and you will receive some useful tips for hatching the eggs and raising healthy hatchlings.

1.) Basic Canary Breeding Info

Before you decide whether or not you want to breed canaries, take a moment to learn the basics about bird breeding. Canaries tend to breed fairly readily in captivity so if you do decide to breed them, all you are likely to have to do is put a male and a female together. Still, you would be wise to familiarize yourself with the canary breeding process first to determine whether or not it is really something you want to do. In this section you will receive some basic information about canary breeding including telling the sexes apart, courtship behavior and nest building behavior exhibited by the species.

a.) Sexual Dimorphism

In order to be successful in breeding canaries you need to pair a male and a female together. If you are new to bird keeping, it can be a challenge to tell males apart from females. For the most part, canaries are not sexually dimorphic – this means that there are not any significant physical differences between the sexes. There are, however, a few subtle things to look for. The first is singing – only males of the species actually sing. Male canaries generally develop this behavior by the time they are 6 months old.

Female canaries might chirp and cheep, but they do not exhibit the same singing ability as a male canary.

In addition to singing, male canaries also tend to have larger bellies that protrude downward toward the legs. Female canaries have more rounded abdomens and their vent tends to lay flat against the body. Male canaries sometimes exhibit a nipple-like protrusion of the vent which prevents it from lying flat. This protrusion becomes more evident during breeding season.

b.) Courtship Behavior

Male canaries sing to attract a mate, so singing is an important part of courtship behavior. You may find, however, that if you keep a female and a male canary together that the male will stop singing because he has already found a mate. The breeding season for canaries begins in the spring, though males may begin to prepare for breeding a few weeks before the females as winter is just ending. If you keep a male and female canary together, the male may start to chase the female around the cage at this time. Keep a close eye on your canaries at this point because the male can become aggressive.

To prevent problems, it is best to house your male and female canary separately until the female is ready to breed. In female canaries, building a nest is the best indicator that the female is ready to breed. For males, courtship behavior may include feeding the female and "kissing" her. If the sexes are separated, the male may make visual displays in addition to singing. You will know that the two are ready to mate when the female acknowledges the displays of the male – she will indicated this by crouching down to allow mating to occur.

c.) Nest Building

If you plan to breed your canaries, it is best to keep them in separate cages until they are both ready for breeding. In females, the sign that she is ready for breeding is that she will build a nest. For the best results, you should house the female in the cage you want to use as your breeding cage so you do not have to move her or the nest after it has been built. The ideal dimensions for a canary breeding cage are 18x11x14 inches (46x28x36 cm). Provide the female with a wicker or wooden nesting box and a pan of nesting materials. Recommended nesting materials include soft wood shavings, small twigs, and other soft bedding materials.

2.) The Canary Breeding Process

Once the female canary has built her nest you can introduce the male canary. In most cases, breeding occurs very soon after the pair are introduced – you shouldn't have to do anything to encourage the two to breed. Just be sure that the canaries are the right age for breeding before you begin the process. Female canaries should be at least 1 year old for breeding and male canaries should be no more than 5 years old. Sexual maturity for canaries typically occurs around 9 months of age, though it could be sooner for some male canaries.

While preparing your canaries for breeding you should feed them a healthy diet with rich foods. For females, you want to make sure that she gets enough fats and oils to prevent constipation and egg binding – adding a little bit of olive oil or wheat germ oil to her seed should help with this. Once the pair are both ready for breeding you can introduce the male to the female's cage – do not do it the other way around.

After a successful mating, the female will lay one egg per day until she is finished. Canaries can lay up to 6 eggs per clutch, though the average is 3 to 5 eggs. Once the eggs have been laid the female will incubate them for about 13 to 14 days before they hatch. In some cases you may notice the female taking a bath the day of or before hatching. When she returns to the nest she will wet the bedding which will help to soften the eggs in preparation for hatching. When the chicks are ready to hatch they will start by chipping a small hole in the side of the egg and then keep chipping away until the egg splits open.

When canary chicks first hatch they are almost completely naked and wet. The chicks eyes will be closed and their beaks will be soft so they are completely dependent on the hen for care. The chicks will likely subsist off of the remainder of their yolk sac for half a day or so but they will need to be fed within 24 hours of hatching. In many cases, both the male and female canary care for the chicks, though some recommend removing the male from the cage after breeding just to be safe.

To make sure that your canary chicks get enough to eat you can start offering nestling food or you can make your own using mashed hardboiled eggs with water-soaked whole wheat bread. The female will continue to feed and care for the chicks until they are about 21 days old at which point they will leave the nest and begin to live independently. When the chicks are fully weaned they should be separated from the parents.

Chapter Seven: Keeping Canaries Healthy

Feeding your pet canary a healthy diet is the best thing you can do to keep him healthy but it will not necessarily protect him from disease. You cannot always predict when your canary might get sick but you can equip yourself with knowledge about common canary diseases so you know how to handle them if they should arise. In this chapter you will receive an overview of common conditions affecting canaries as well as tips for preventing disease and quarantining new birds. Using the information in this chapter you can keep your canary as healthy as possible for as long as possible.

1.) Common Health Problems

Canaries are bright and energetic little birds that can be extremely entertaining to keep as pets. Unfortunately, canaries are prone to a number of different diseases which can impact their health and wellbeing. If you want to make sure that your canary gets the care he needs if he falls ill, you would be wise to familiarize yourself with some of the most common health problems known to affect the species. You will find a list of the most common conditions known to affect canaries below and, in the following pages, you will receive an overview of these conditions including causes, symptoms, and treatment options.

Common conditions known to affect canaries may include the following:

- Air Sac Mites
- Aspergillosis
- Canary Pox
- Egg Binding

- Feather Cysts
- Feather Loss
- Scaly Mites
- Tapeworms

Air Sac Mites

Respiratory problems are not uncommon in pet canaries and one of the most frequently seen respiratory issues is related to a parasite infection known as air sac mites. Air sac mites can infiltrate the bird's entire respiratory tract and the severity of the infection can vary greatly. Birds with mild infections may not show any signs but severe infections may produce symptoms including trouble breathing, wheezing or clicking sounds, open-mouth breathing, excessive salivation, and bobbing the tail. Canaries with air sac mites often stop singing and many exhibit reduced activity and puffed feathers.

Unfortunately, diagnosing a live bird with air sac mites can be difficult. In some cases the mites might be visible to the naked eye, though a microscope is usually needed to make a diagnosis after a tracheal swab. This disease can be transmitted through close contact with an infected bird and through airborne particles. It can also be passed through contaminated food or drinking water so it is important that you quarantine your canary from other birds if it displays signs of air sac mites.

There are some treatment options available for air sac mites but you need to be very careful about choosing the right treatment. The signs that indicate air sac mites overlap with a number of other diseases so you need to make sure you have an accurate diagnosis before you start treatment. For example, vitamin A deficiency presents with symptoms very similar to air sac mites. Medications are available to treat the disease, though dosage can be tricky and many birds die from air sac mites.

Aspergillosis

Another common respiratory problem seen in pet birds like the canary is aspergillosis. This is a disease caused by a fungus and it is a slow-growing infection that can cause serious tissue damage throughout the body. Unfortunately, there is little physical evidence of a problem until the disease has progressed and the damage to the internal organs becomes severe. Not only is this disease difficult to detect, but it can also be very challenging to treat and to cure.

Aspergillosis can affect both the upper and lower respiratory tract. This fungus can be found in many environments but it doesn't typically become a problem until the bird's immune system becomes compromised by something else. Chronic stress, poor husbandry, and other respiratory irritants can increase a canary's risk for contracting this fungal infection. Once the bird gets sick, curing the infection can take a long time.

Because aspergillosis frequently presents without symptoms it can be difficult to diagnose. Your vet will likely recommend a complete blood count (CBC), an x-ray to check for lesions, and a tracheal wash to detect the presence of the fungus in the respiratory tract. Treatment options include oral or intravenous antifungal medications which must be taken over an extended period of time. Unfortunately, treatment is often ineffective unless the bird's immune system is very strong. This is fairly uncommon, however, because the disease tends to attack birds with compromised immune systems. If you do manage to cure the disease it is important that you maintain good hygiene and a healthy diet to prevent the disease from recurring or spreading.

Canary Pox

Also known as canary pox virus (CNPV), canary pox is one strain of a virus that can affect a wide variety of different bird species. The umbrella name for this condition is Avian Pox. Canary pox is typically transmitted by mites or mosquitoes and it is particularly common in birds that are housed outdoors. It is also possible for the disease to be transmitted through inhalation of airborne droplets or by eating infected scabs. Even after recovering from the disease, a canary can still be a carrier of canary pox and can pass it to other birds.

There are two main types of canary pox – the dry form and the wet form. The dry form produces crusted areas on the skin as well as lesions and feather loss. The wet form produces thickened plaques in the mouth, throat, and sinuses. Other symptoms which may accompany canary pox include rapid breathing, weight loss, listlessness, puffed feathers, and sudden death.

Unfortunately, these symptoms overlap with many other diseases so canary pox can be tricky to diagnose. It is also unfortunately true that canary pox has no cure and it is fatal in about 80% of cases. There are no medications available to combat the virus but some treatments can help to manage symptoms. Proper hygiene and avoiding contact with wild birds is the key to preventing this disease.

Egg Binding

Egg binding is a condition that can occur in any female bird and it is very dangerous and frequently fatal. This condition occurs when the egg fails to pass through the reproductive system at the normal rate. Female canaries can develop this condition regardless of the presence of a male since birds still lay eggs whether or not they are fertilized. Another dangerous and related condition is dystocia – this occurs when an obstruction prevents the female bird from laying the egg.

There are a number of factors which can increase your canary's risk for egg binding. Egg binding is particularly common in small birds like canaries and repeated breeding (as well as breeding too young or out of season) can also be a factor. Egg binding is common in very young and very old birds, plus it can be affected by issues with malnutrition or poor overall health.

Egg binding is incredibly serious and frequently fatal so it is important that you are able to recognize the signs. Symptoms of egg binding may include abdominal straining, bobbing the tail, drooping wings, depression, loss of appetite, leg paralysis, distended abdomen, difficulty breathing, and sudden death. If you suspect egg binding, seek veterinary care immediately for your canary.

Feather Cysts

In the same way that humans can develop ingrown hairs, canaries can develop feather cysts. Feather cysts form when the growing feather is malformed within the follicle (the part located under the skin) – it happens when the growing feather is unable to protrude through the skin so it curls up inside the follicle. This produces an oval-shaped or elongated swelling that can develop anywhere on the wing, though they are most common near the primary feathers. Canaries can also develop feather cysts on the body.

Feather cysts may be small and minor at first but as they grow they can accumulate a yellowish-white keratin material that fills the cyst. Cysts can develop as a result of several factors including bacterial and viral infections, trauma, malnutrition, self-mutilation, and other problems related to feather growth. Feather cysts can affect any canary but they are most common in Border canaries, Norwich canaries, and Glosters.

If the feather cyst is very small it can sometimes be squeezed out. This is not the ideal treatment, however, because the cyst may reform. Feather cysts have the potential to bleed profusely so they are best handled by a qualified avian veterinarian. Surgical removal may be the only option in some cases.

Feather Loss

In canaries and other related species, stress is the most common cause for feather loss. When your canary becomes stressed due to an aggressive cage mate, poor hygiene, or an unhealthy diet he may start plucking out his own feathers. Another potential cause for feather loss is parasite infection. Some birds also experience feather loss as the result of an iodine deficiency, though this is more common in Gouldian finches than in canaries. If the feather loss is limited to the head, it is most likely due to aggression by other birds or a mite infection.

Scaly Mites

Mites belonging to the genus *Knemidokoptes* are common referred to as "scaly mites" and they can affect the legs and face of multiple bird species. When scaly mites affect the legs it is sometimes called Tassel Foot. Scaly mites are particularly common in small birds like the canary and they typically cause scaly, crusty white or gray lesions on the non-feathered skin on the beak, legs, and feet. Foot lesions are particularly common in canaries, though they can also appear around the eyes and vent.

The parasites known as scaly mites typically spend their entire life cycles on the bird they are inhabiting. The mites burrow into the top layer of skin, forming tunnels they can travel through. The mites can be transmitted from one bird to another through direct contact – they can also be transferred to un-feathered chicks. If the bird has a suppressed immune system it has a greater susceptibility to contracting the disease.

There are several treatment options available for scaly mites but the most effective treatment is Ivermectin. This treatment is usually administered at 10-day intervals for 2 to 6 treatments. Ivermectin can be applied directly to the skin or it can be taken orally or injected. In addition to treatment with Ivermectin, the cage and all accessories need to be cleaned and disinfected.

Tapeworms

Tapeworms are a type of internal parasite that most commonly affects birds that are kept outdoors. These parasites can be transmitted to your canary if they eat an infected insect or through contact with contaminated feces. Once the tapeworm makes it into the bird's digestive tract it starts to leech nutrients, causing the bird to develop malnutrition. As the tapeworm grows and multiplies it can also produce a physical blockage of the intestinal tract which can become fatal for the bird.

Unfortunately, many birds affected by tapeworms do not show any outward symptoms until the malnutrition becomes fairly advanced. In some cases, however, you can actually see shed tapeworms in the bird's droppings if you look closely. A fecal exam is the best method for diagnosing a tapeworm infection and once your bird is diagnosed your vet will prescribe an anti-parasitic medication. These medications can be administered orally or through injection depending on the severity of the condition.

2.) *Preventing Illness*

In addition to familiarizing yourself with common canary diseases, there are some other steps you can take to prevent illness. The most important thing you need to do is to keep your canary cage clean. Below you will find an overview of recommended daily, weekly, and monthly cleaning tasks for your canary cage.

Daily Cleaning Tasks

On a daily basis you should replace your canary cage liner, clean your food and water dishes, and clean and refresh your bird bath. You may also want to clean your canary's toys and accessories if they become soiled. Because your cage liner should be changed daily you might want to use newspaper to line the cage instead of buying cage liners – this will save you a lot of money. Another time-saving trick is to put several layers of newspaper down on the bottom of your canary cage. Then, when it is time for cleaning, you can just remove the top layer.

When it comes to cleaning your food and water bowls as well as your bird bath you need to clean as well as disinfect the object. Clean the dishes in hot soapy water then rinse well. To disinfect, dip the dishes in a mixture of ½ cup of bleach to 1 gallon of water. Let the dishes soak for 5 to 10 minutes then rinse well and dry completely before refilling them and putting them back in the cage. Daily cleaning and disinfecting is very important.

Weekly/Monthly Cleaning Tasks

In addition to cleaning your canary cage accessories on a daily basis you should clean the whole cage thoroughly about once a week. If you keep a single canary you might be able to wait and clean the cage only every other week or even once a month. For multiple canaries, however, it is best to clean the cage weekly. To do this you will need to remove your canary to a safe place – you'll want to keep a backup cage around for this purpose.

To clean the cage, remove everything that is not permanently attached and clean the items individually using hot, soapy water. Again, disinfect everything with a bleach solution then rinse well and dry them completely. To clean the cage itself you should use a bird-friendly disinfectant spray and wipe down the entire cage. Once the accessories are cleaned, disinfected, and dried you can reassemble the cage.

3.) Quarantining/Introducing New Birds

If you plan to keep multiple canaries together in the same cage, your best bet is to purchase them while they are still young and to raise them together. If you start out with a single canary and decide later on that you want another, you will need to quarantine the new bird before introducing it in order to make sure that the new addition doesn't introduce any disease. Below you will find some tips for quarantining new birds:

- Quarantining is ALWAYS recommended for new birds – this practice should not be reserved for breeders.

- The new bird should be completely isolated during quarantine – keep it in an entirely separate room, if possible.

- Shut off air conditioning/heating to and from the quarantine room to avoid airborne contamination – you may have to draw in fresh air from the outside using a fan.

- Keep a close eye on your bird during the quarantine period to check for any signs of illness – refer to the information from the beginning of this chapter for symptoms.

- Maintain the quarantine long enough to ensure that any disease finishes its incubation period – this could take as long as six weeks.

- During the quarantine, be very careful not to share accessories or tools between the two cages – you should also be careful about changing your clothes and washing your hands.

- Only if your bird shows zero signs of disease after the six week quarantine can it be considered safe to introduce him to your other canary.

If your new bird successfully makes it through the quarantine period without incident you can take the necessary steps to introduce him to your other canary. Again, this is a process that should not be rushed for the safety and wellbeing of both birds. You can start by placing the two cages in the same room so the birds can get used to each other from afar. You can slowly move the cages closer together over a period of several weeks and give the birds limited time together in a shared flight cage.

When you are ready to permanently combine the birds, make sure the cage is thoroughly cleaned and arranged so that each bird can have its own territory. Refer to the information in Chapter Five about keeping multiple canaries together to determine the right size cage for keeping more than one canary.

Chapter Eight: Canary Care Sheet

In reading this book you have received a wealth of information about the canary. Using this information you will not only be equipped to decide whether the canary is the right pet for you, but you will also learn what it takes to be the best canary owner you can be. If you do decide to get a canary, you will always have the information in this book to fall back on. If you find yourself with a specific question, you may not want to go back through the whole book to find it. That is why in this chapter you will find a canary care sheet with all of the most important facts including tips for cage set-up, feeding, and breeding.

1.) Basic Information

- **Classification**: *Serinus canaria domestica*
- **Taxonomy**: order Passeriformes, family Fringillidae, genus Serinus, species *Serinus canaria*
- **Distribution**: Macaronesian Islands (Canary Islands, Morocco, Azores, and Madeira)
- **Habitat**: forested areas, primarily pine and laurel forests; also man-made habitats
- **Anatomical Adaptations**:
- **Eggs**: up to 5 per clutch, average is 3 to 4; 2 to 3 broods per year
- **Incubation Period**: average 13 to 14 days
- **Hatchling**: young birds leave the next after 14 to 21 days, average 15 to 17 days
- **Average Size**: 4 to 4.7 inches in length (10 to 12 cm)
- **Average Weight**: 15 grams (0.53 oz.)
- **Wingspan**: about 8 to 9 inches (20 to 23 cm)
- **Coloration**: wide variety of colors; yellow, white, orange, red, black, brown, etc.
- **Sexual Dimorphism**: male is more brightly colored; female has a greyer head
- **Diet**: mostly seeds, small insects, and other plant materials
- **Vocalization**: silvery twittering, similar to finches
- **Lifespan**: average 10 to 15 years

2.) Cage Set-up Guide

- **Minimum Cage Dimensions**: 18 by 18 by 24 inches (46x46x61 cm) for a single bird; larger for a pair or multiple birds
- **Cage Shape**: longer is better to accommodate natural flight pattern; flight cages are ideal
- **Minimum Height**: 18 inches (46 cm)
- **Bar Spacing**: no more than ½ inch
- **Required Accessories**: food and water dishes, perches, bathing tub, nesting box/materials, cuttlebone, toys
- **Food/Water Dish**: at least one per bird; made from stainless steel, ceramic, or other heavy duty materials
- **Positioning Dishes**: space them throughout the cage
- **Perches**: at least three in different locations; stagger heights to accommodate flight; no completely smooth or sandpaper perches
- **Recommended Toys**: rope toys, stainless steel bells, swings, etc.; keep an assortment with at least 3 toys in the cage at all times; rotate often
- **Bathing Tub:** heavy duty materials, 1 to 2 inches water; on floor of cage or mounted to the side
- **Nests**: nesting box made from wood or bamboo; mounted to side or back of the cage near the top
- **Nesting Materials**: soft wood shavings, small twigs, other soft materials

- **Materials for Homemade Cage**: plywood top and bottom, 1-by-2 inch supports, welded wire mesh enclosure
- **Recommended Temperature Range**: warm temperatures, between 60°F and 70°F (15.5°C to 21°C), no more than 78°F (25.5°C); nighttime temperature no lower than 40°F (4.5°C)
- **Humidity:** doesn't need to be too high, between 50% to 60% is adequate; higher humidity may be beneficial for breeding

3.) Nutritional Information

- **Diet in the Wild**: primarily seeds, some small insects and other plant matter
- **Diet in Captivity**: 60% to 70% seeds, 30% to 40% fresh vegetables, fruits, grains, and protein
- **Protein**: cooked chicken egg, mealworms, other insects
- **Carbohydrate**: whole grain bread, whole wheat bread, cooked brown rice, cooked potato, cooked sweet potato, fresh fruits and vegetables
- **Fats**: seeds, some insects
- **Minerals**: supplement diet with cuttlebone and/or oyster grit; powdered multivitamin optional
- **Recommended Diet Structure:**

- **Supplementary Foods**: fresh vegetables daily, fruit 3 times per week, cooked grains/starch and protein 2 times per week
- **Feeding Amount**: 1 to 2 teaspoons seed daily; follow feeding recommendations on pellet package; small amounts of supplementary foods
- **Feeding Tips**: one food dish per bird, spaced throughout the cage; shallow dishes, clean daily; offer fresh water at all times

4.) Breeding Tips

- **Sexual Dimorphism**: males are better singers; females have rounded abdomen and flat-lying vent; males have larger bellies and nipple-like protrusion on the vent
- **Seasonal Changes**: breeding season begins in the spring
- **Sexual Maturity**: around 9 months
- **Breeding Age (male)**: under 5 years old
- **Breeding Age (female)**: at least 1 year old
- **Preparing for Breeding**: house male and female in separate cages next to each other for several weeks
- **Breeding Cage**: about 18x11x14 inches (46x28x36 cm); equipped with pan of nesting materials; breeding box/nest made of wicker or wood

- **Recommended Nesting Materials**: soft wood shavings, small twigs, other soft bedding materials
- **Courtship Behavior**: female begins to build the nest, male starts to court the female at onset of breeding season; if female is willing, she will crouch down and allow for mating
- **Egg Laying**: female lays one egg per day; eggs are blue-green in color with brown speckling
- **Clutch Size**: 3 to 5 eggs per clutch, as many as 6 is possible
- **Incubation Period**: 13 to 14 days on average
- **Hatching**: female might take a bath and return to the nest to wet the eggs, softening them for hatching
- **Raising Chicks**: both parents tend to care for the chicks
- **Fledging**: chicks typically leave the nest around day 21
- **Breeding Frequency**: average 2 to 3 clutches per year

Chapter Nine: Relevant Websites

Now that you have finished this book you should have a much deeper understanding of what it takes to be a canary owner. If you have decided that the canary is indeed the right pet for you, your next move is to buy the necessary equipment and set up your cage to get it ready for your new pet! In this chapter you will find a collection of useful resources to help you get off on the right track in choosing your canary's cage, cage accessories, food, and more.

1. Canary Cage Links

Below you will find a collection of helpful resources and websites for canary cages. Remember, your canary will spend most of his life in his cage so it is important that you choose the right one!

United States Links:

Cages By Design. <http://www.cagesbydesign.com/t-flightcage.aspx>

King's Cages. <http://www.kingscages.com/SearchResults.aspx?CategoryID=Cages&SubCatID=Canary,%20Finch,%20Parakeet,%20Sugar%20Glider%20Cages>

Bird Cages 4 Less. <http://birdcages4less.com/page/B/CTGY/Canary-Bird-Cages>

PetSolutions – Small Bird Cages. <http://www.petsolutions.com/C/Small-Bird-Cages-Canaries-Finches-Parakeets+SAll.aspx>

Canary Advisor – The Canary Cage.
<http://www.canaryadvisor.com/canary-cage.html>

United Kingdom Links:

Cages World – Canary Bird Cages.
<http://www.cagesworld.co.uk/c/Canary_Bird_Cages.htm>

ZooPlus – Canary Cages.
<http://www.zooplus.co.uk/shop/birds/bird_cages_and_acce
ssories/canary_cages>

Scarlett's Parrot Essentials – Flight Cage.
<http://www.scarlettsparrotessentials.co.uk/flight-cage/>

Seapets – Budgie, Canary, and Finch Cages.
<https://www.seapets.co.uk/bird-supplies/bird-
cages/budgie-cages-canary-and-finch-cages>

2. Canary Cage Accessories and Toys

Below you will find a collection of websites for canary cage accessories including food and water dishes, perches, toys, and more.

United States Links:

Drs. Foster and Smith – Bird Cage Accessories.
<http://www.drsfostersmith.com/bird-supplies/bird-cage-accessories/ps/c/5059/11295>

King's Cages – Canary Supplies. <http://www.kingscages.com/SearchResults.aspx?CategoryID=Canary%5EFinch%20Breeding%20Supplies,%20Cuttle%20Bone>

PetSmart – Toys, Perches, & Décor.
<http://www.petsmart.com/bird/toys-perches-decor/cat-36-catid-400010>

Glamorous Gouldians – Bird Cage Supplies & Accessories.
<http://glamgouldians.com/shop-cage.php>

United Kingdom Links:

ZooPlus – Bird Cage Accessories.
<http://www.zooplus.co.uk/shop/birds/cage_accessories>

Scarlett's Parrot Essentials – Perches.
<http://www.scarlettsparrotessentials.co.uk/perches>

Seapets – Bird Toys. <https://www.seapets.co.uk/bird-supplies/bird-toys>

Cages World – Cage Accessories.
<http://www.cagesworld.co.uk/c/Bird_Cage_Accessories.ht m>

3. Canary Diet and Food Links

Below you will find a collection of useful resources and websites to help you craft the ideal diet for your canary.

United States Links:

Dr. Harvey's Incredible Canary Blend.
<https://www.drharveys.com/products/birds/341-incredible-canary-blend-natural-food-for-canaries>

Lafeber – Canary Pellets. <https://lafeber.com/pet-birds/birdfood/canary-pellets/>

Dr. Foster and Smith – Finch/Canary Food. <http://www.drsfostersmith.com/bird-supplies/food-formulas-diets/finch-canary-food-diets/ps/c/5059/5911/5912>

Haith's – Canary and British Seed Mixes. <http://www.haiths.com/cage-and-aviary-bird-seed/canary-and-british/>

United Kingdom Links:

Seapets – Canary and Finch Treats. <https://www.seapets.co.uk/bird-supplies/bird-toys/canary-and-finch-treats>

Buckton's Canary Seed. <http://www.bucktons.co.uk/products/canary-seed/>

ZooPlus – Canary Food. <http://www.zooplus.co.uk/shop/birds/bird_food/canary_food>

Index

A

accessories 23, 44, 47, 48, 81, 83, 84, 85, 87, 96, 98, 99, 100
activity 39, 50, 73
age 23, 60, 68
aggression 80
Air Sac Mites 72, 73
ancestor 4
animal movement license... 33
Aspergillosis 72, 75
Atlantic canary 7, 9
Avian Pox 77

B

baby 3, 4
bacteria 44, 45
basket 91
beak 47, 81
behavior 62, 65, 66, 67
belly 7, 10
berries 52
bird bath 24, 45, 83, 84
bite.. 29, 61
bond... 5
breeder 30, 34, 35, 36, 39, 40
breeding..... 3, 2, 5, 6, 7, 10, 19, 35, 36, 49, 64, 65, 66, 67, 68, 69, 78, 89, 92, 94

C

cage .19, 21, 23, 24, 26, 27, 29, 40, 41, 42, 43, 44, 45, 46, 47, 48, 49, 50, 52, 57, 60, 61, 63, 66, 67, 69, 80, 81, 83, 84, 85, 86, 87, 88, 89, 91, 93, 96, 97, 98, 99, 100, 101, 115

cage liners 43, 84

calcium...47, 54, 55

canary 3, 1, 2, 6, 7, 8, 9, 10, 11, 13, 15, 17, 18, 19, 21, 23, 24, 25, 26, 27, 30, 32, 34, 35, 36, 37, 39, 40, 41, 42, 43, 44, 45, 46, 47, 48, 49, 50, 51, 52, 53, 55, 56, 57, 58, 59, 60, 61, 62, 63, 65, 66, 67, 68, 69, 70, 71, 72, 73, 75, 77, 78, 79, 80, 81, 82, 83, 84, 86, 87, 88, 89, 96, 97, 98, 99, 101, 102, 111, 115, 116, 117

Canary Islands 9, 11, 12, 13, 90

Canary Pox 72, 77

captivity 7, 11, 46, 65

carbohydrates 53, 56

care...3, 2, 25, 26, 64, 69, 70, 72, 78, 89, 95

cats 21

causes 4, 72

chick.. 4

chicks 69, 70, 81, 95

classification.. 5

cleaning..25, 26, 43, 52, 83, 84

clutch 11, 12, 69, 90, 94

color.. 1, 7, 8, 10, 11, 15, 16, 40, 94

color canaries 8, 15, 16

coloration...1, 7, 10

conditions 14, 71, 72

conformations..8, 15

cost 18, 23, 24, 25, 26

courtship..65, 66, 67

cuttlebone.. 47, 54, 55, 91, 93

D

death..77, 78 diagnosis 73, 74

diet........................ 6, 10, 23, 25, 41, 51, 52, 53, 57, 68, 71, 76, 80, 93, 101, 117

diseases...33, 71, 72, 73, 77, 83

dishes.. 24, 44, 57, 83, 84, 91, 93, 99

DIY canary cage 48

dogs 13, 21

domesticated 1, 7, 8

dominance 19

droppings 82

dystocia.. 78

E

egg 4

Egg Binding...72, 78

eggs.. 3, 4, 11, 31, 49, 64, 69, 70, 78, 94, 95

environment 114

equipment 96

estrildid finches 12, 90

Estrildidae 11, 90

European serin 13

eyes..40, 69, 81

F

family 5

fat 53

feather 16, 35, 77, 79, 80

Feather Cysts..72, 79

Feather Loss 72, 80

feathers...3, 4, 5

feeding...3, 2, 22, 41, 51, 52, 56, 57, 58, 67, 89, 93, 114

female.............................. 3, 5, 12, 64, 65, 66, 67, 68, 69, 70, 78, 90, 94, 95

finch 1, 7, 19, 21, 29, 31, 98, 101, 102, 116

flight..19, 24, 42, 46, 47, 48, 63, 87, 91, 98

flight cage 19, 24, 43
follicle 79
food ... 24, 25, 40, 44, 52, 53, 56, 57, 58, 70, 73, 83, 84, 91, 93, 96, 99, 101, 102
fruits 25, 52, 54, 55, 57, 58, 93
fungal 75

G

genus 7, 12, 13, 81, 90
grains 52, 53, 93
grit 55, 93
grooming... 23, 24

H

habitat 6, 13, 23, 41, 42, 49, 117
handling 22, 41, 62
hatched.. 3, 4
hatching 11, 49, 64, 69, 95
health... 30, 36, 40, 63, 72, 78, 114
history.. 4
humidity.. 49, 92, 115
husbandry 75
hygiene 76, 77, 80

I

illness 39, 40, 83, 86
immune system... 75, 76, 81
incubate 69
infection.. 73, 75, 80, 82
initial costs 23
insects... 10, 12, 52, 54, 90, 93
Ivermectin 81

L

larvae 93

lesions 75, 77, 81

license 31, 32, 35

lifespan 11

M

maintenance 29

male 5, 12, 19, 64, 65, 66, 68, 69, 78, 90, 94, 111

malnutrition 78, 79, 82

mandibles 3

maturity 68

Migratory Bird Treaty Act 31, 116

mites 73, 77, 81

multivitamin 55, 93

mutations 8, 15

N

nails 62

nest 4, 10, 11, 26, 46, 65, 66, 67, 68, 69, 70, 94, 95

nesting 5

nesting box 24, 46, 67, 91

nesting materials 26, 46, 67, 94

nutrients 53, 56, 82

nutritional needs 51, 52

O

offspring 3, 4

order 5

P

pair.................................... 10, 19, 23, 25, 65, 68, 69, 91

parakeets 22

parasite 73, 80, 82

parental care 12, 90

parrots 22, 28, 63

passerine 7

pattern 8, 40, 91

pellet 25, 53, 58, 93

perches 19, 24, 43, 45, 48, 49, 91, 99, 100

permit 30, 31, 32

personality 1

pet store 34

plants 116

population 9

primary feathers.. 79

pros and cons 28

protein 53, 93

puffed 40, 73, 77

Q

quarantine 73, 86, 87

quick 43, 62

R

rabies 33

Red Factor Canary 16

reproductive system... 78

resources 96, 97, 101

respiratory 73, 75

S

Scaly Mites 72, 81
season.. 11, 19, 66, 78, 94
seed mix..25, 45, 53
seeds................................. 10, 12, 51, 52, 53, 54, 55, 56, 57, 58, 90, 93
sexes 5
sexually dimorphic 65
soaked seeds.. 56
society finches.. 22
song 8, 12, 14, 15, 17, 90
song canaries 8, 15, 17
songbirds 7
space...28, 29, 47, 48, 57, 91
species .3, 1, 2, 3, 4, 5, 6, 7, 10, 12, 13, 15, 19, 21, 28, 29, 31, 33, 48, 64, 65, 72, 77, 80, 81, 90, 117
sperm.. 3
stress.. 50, 61, 75, 80
styptic powder 24, 62
symptoms 72, 73, 74, 75, 77, 82, 87

T

tail... 4, 5, 7, 10, 24, 40, 73, 78
tame 60
Tapeworms 72, 82
Tassel Foot 81
temperature.. 49, 50, 56, 92, 115
territory 10, 19, 88
toys 23, 24, 27, 47, 83, 91, 99, 100, 102
training.. 61
treatment.. 72, 73, 76, 79, 81
type..1, 15, 16, 19, 23, 24, 35, 36, 40, 82
type canaries..8, 15, 16

U

U.S Fish and Wildlife Service...32

V

vegetables... 25, 52, 54, 55, 57, 58, 93
vent.. 40, 66, 81, 94
veterinarian...26, 63, 79
virus 77

W

water 24, 40, 44, 45, 49, 52, 55, 56, 58, 70, 73, 83, 84, 85, 91, 92, 93, 99
wild 1, 7, 8, 9, 10, 11, 13, 16, 32, 42, 52, 53, 77
wing 3, 4, 5
wings.. 10, 12, 63, 78, 90
wingspan.. 10

Photo Credits

Cover Photo By Flickr user Majd Mohabek, <https://www.flickr.com/photos/majd192/5341039692/sizes/l>

Page 1 Photo by Flickr user Jacilluch, <https://www.flickr.com/photos/70626035@N00/18832716031/sizes/l>

Page 6 Photo By Flickr user Steve P2008, <https://www.flickr.com/photos/stevepj2009/14994406156/sizes/l>

Page 9 Photo By Juan Emilio via Wikimedia Commons, <https://en.wikipedia.org/wiki/File:Serinus_canaria_-Parque_Rural_del_Nublo,_Gran_Canaria,_Spain_-male-8a.jpg>

Page 15 Photo By Alan Manson via Wikimedia Commons, https://en.wikipedia.org/wiki/Forest_canary#/media/File:Forest_Canary_(Serinus_scotops)_facing_left,_side_view.jpg

Page 18 Photo By Flickr user Greencolander, <https://www.flickr.com/photos/greencolander/1464739966/>

Page 21 Photo By Flickr user Micolo J Thankx 4, <https://www.flickr.com/photos/robin1966/16002396894/sizes/h/>

Page 28 Photo By Juan Emilio via Wikimedia Commons, <https://en.wikipedia.org/wiki/File:Serinus_canaria_-Gran_Canaria,_Canary_Islands,_Spain-8_(1).jpg>

Page 30 Photo By Flickr user Steve P2008, <https://www.flickr.com/photos/stevepj2009/15014577471/sizes/l>

Page 34 Photo By Flickr user Roberto Composto, <https://www.flickr.com/photos/robertocomposto/4570498366/sizes/l>

Page 41 Photo By Flickr user Majd Mohabek, <https://www.flickr.com/photos/majd192/5340873446/sizes/l>

Page 51 Photo By Jorg Hempel via Wikimedia Commons, <https://de.wikipedia.org/wiki/Kanarengirlitz#/media/File:Serinus_canaria_LC0210.jpg>

Page 64 Photo By Fir0002 via Wikimedia Commons, <https://en.wikipedia.org/wiki/File:Canary_nesting.jpg>

Page 68 Photo 19

Page 71 Photo By Flickr user Newtown Grafitti, <https://www.flickr.com/photos/newtown_grafitti/52574155 32/sizes/l>

Page 83 Photo By Flickr user Azzam Daaboul, <https://www.flickr.com/photos/ec1ipze/16865847948/sizes/l >

Page 89 Photo By Flickr user Rkramer62, <https://www. flickr.com/photos/rkramer62/6827032314/sizes/l>

Page 96 Photo By Flickr user David.R.Carroll, <https://www.flickr.com/photos/david_carroll/2789498823/si zes/l>

References

"A List of the Orders of the Class Aves: Birds." Earthlife.net.
   <http://www.earthlife.net/birds/orders.html>

"Bird Cage Cleaning: Daily, Weekly, and Monthly Bird Cage
   Maintenance." PetEducation.com. <http://www.peteducation.
   com/article.cfm?c=15+1794&aid=2837>

"Bird Terminology." Birds of North America. <http://www.birds-
   of-north-america.net/Bird_Terminology.html>

"Birds You Don't Need a License to Keep." Office of Environment
   and Heritage. <http://www.environment.nsw.
   gov.au/wildlifelicences/BirdsYouDontNeedALicenceToKeep.h
   tm>

"Breeding Canaries." Aria from a Bird Cage.
   <http://www.ariafromabirdcage.com/Breeding.htm>

"Breeding Canaries." Beauty of Birds.
   <https://www.beautyofbirds.com/canarybreeding.html>

"Canaries." Pet Supplies Plus. <http://www.petsuppliesplus.com/
   content.jsp?pageName=canaries>

"Canaries: Small Songbirds in the Finch Family." Beauty of Birds.
   <https://www.beautyofbirds.com/canaryinfo.html>

"Canaries – Feeding." VCA Animal Hospitals.
   <http://www.vcahospitals.com/main/pet-health-
   information/article/animal-health/canaries-feeding/808>

"Canary Bird Cage Buyer's Guide." Bird-Cage.com.
   <http://www.bird-cage.com/canary-cages>

"Canary Care – About Canaries." Animal-World.com.
<http://animal-world.com/encyclo/birds/canaries/
CanaryProfile.htm>

"Canary Nutrition." Topflite. <http://topflite.co.nz/tips/canary-
nutrition/>

"Choosing a Healthy Bird." About Home. <http://birds.about.
com/od/adoptingabird/a/babybirds.htm>

"Common Finch Diseases." Beauty of Birds.
<https://www.beautyofbirds.com/finchdiseases.html>

"Cost of Owning a Bird: Setup, Supplies, and Veterinary Care."
PetEducation.com. <http://www.peteducation.com/
article.cfm?c=15+1794&aid=1516>

"Grooming Pet Birds: How to Clip Wings, Trim Beaks and Nails,
and Bathe Your Bird." PetEducation.com. <http://www.
peteducation.com/article.cfm?c=15+1794&aid=180>

"How to Build a Bird Cage." Pet Care GT. <http://www.
petcaregt.com/petcare/howtobuildabirdcage.html>

"Ideal Lighting, Temperature, and Humidity." Finch Information
Center. <http://www.finchinfo.com/housing/lighting_
temperature_humidity.php>

"Inspecting and Choosing a Healthy Bird." Psittacine Breeding &
Research Farm. <http://www.parrotpro.com/inspect.php>

"List of Migratory Bird Species Protected by the Migratory Bird
Treaty Act as of December 2, 2013." U.S. Fish & Wildlife
Service Migratory Bird Program. <http://www.fws.gov/
migratorybirds/RegulationsPolicies/mbta/MBTANDX.HTML

"Nail Clipping." Finch Aviary. <http://www.finchaviary.com/ Maintenance/NailClipping.htm>

"Permits." U.S. Fish & Wildlife Service Migratory Bird Program. <http://www.fws.gov/migratorybirds/mbpermits.html>

"Pros and Cons of Buying a Canary or Other Pet Finch." Students with Birds. <https://studentswithbirds.wordpress.com/2013/ 12/22/pros-and-cons-of-buying-a-canary-or-other-pet-finch/>

"Safe Plants and Toxic Plants." Finch Information Center. <http://www.finchinfo.com/housing/safe_and_toxic_plants.ph p>

"The Migratory Bird Treaty Act of 1918." Maryland Department of Natural Resources. <http://www.dnr.state.md.us/wildlife/ Plants_Wildlife/MBirdTreatyAct.asp>

"Types of Canaries." Bird Channel.com. <http://www.birdchannel.com/bird-magazines/bird-talk/archives/articles/find-the-right-bird-2004-08-30-1794.aspx>

Feeding Baby
Cynthia Cherry
978-1941070000

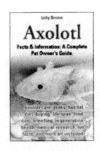

Axolotl
Lolly Brown
978-0989658430

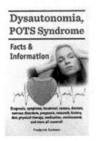

Dysautonomia, POTS
Syndrome
Frederick Earlstein
978-0989658485

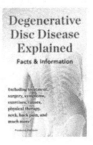

Degenerative Disc
Disease Explained
Frederick Earlstein
978-0989658485

Sinusitis, Hay Fever,
Allergic Rhinitis Explained
Frederick Earlstein
978-1941070024

Wicca
Riley Star
978-1941070130

Zombie Apocalypse
Rex Cutty
978-1941070154

Capybara
Lolly Brown
978-1941070062

Eels As Pets
Lolly Brown
978-1941070167

Scabies and Lice Explained
Frederick Earlstein
978-1941070017

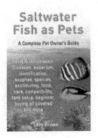

Saltwater Fish As Pets
Lolly Brown
978-0989658461

Torticollis Explained
Frederick Earlstein
978-1941070055

Kennel Cough
Lolly Brown
978-0989658409

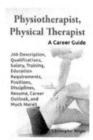

Physiotherapist, Physical
Therapist
Christopher Wright
978-0989658492

Rats, Mice, and Dormice
As Pets
Lolly Brown
978-1941070079

Wallaby and Wallaroo Care
Lolly Brown
978-1941070031

Bodybuilding Supplements
Explained
Jon Shelton
978-1941070239

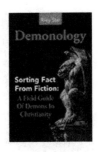

Demonology
Riley Star
978-19401070314

Pigeon Racing
Lolly Brown
978-1941070307

Dwarf Hamster
Lolly Brown
978-1941070390

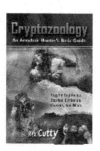

Cryptozoology
Rex Cutty
978-1941070406

Eye Strain
Frederick Earlstein
978-1941070369

Inez The Miniature Elephant
Asher Ray
978-1941070353

Vampire Apocalypse
Rex Cutty
978-1941070321